Psychic Vampires

How To Protect and Heal Yourself From Energy Predators

By

Kelly Wallace

Professional Psychic Counselor

DrKellyPsychic.com[1]

© 2015, 2017, 2021 All Rights Reserved

Intuitive Living Publishing

---

1. *http://DrKellyPsychic.com/*

Table of Contents

Books by Kelly Wallace

10 Minutes A Day to A Powerful New Life

Become Your Higher Self – Using Spiritual Energy to Transform Your Life

Breaking The Worry Habit – Stop Your Anxious Thoughts And Start Living!

Chakras – Heal, Clear, And Strengthen Your Energy Centers

Clear Your Karma – The Healing Power of Your Past Lives

Contacting Your Spirit Guides – Meeting and Working with Your Invisible Helpers

Creating A Charmed Life   Enchantments to Attract, Repel, Cleanse & Heal

Dream Work – Using The Wisdom Of Your Sleeping Mind To Change Your Waking Life

Energy Work – Heal, Cleanse, and Strengthen Your Aura

Everyday Miracles – Powerful Steps to Wonderful Experiences

Finding Your Life Purpose – Uncover Your Soul's True Goals

Healing the Child Within – Rewrite Your Early Childhood Life Script

How to Cure Candida – Yeast Infection Symptoms, Causes, Diet & Natural Remedies

Intuitive Living – Developing Your Psychic Gifts

Intuitive Tarot – Learn the Tarot Instantly

Is He The One? Finding And Keeping Your Soulmate

Master the Art of Picking Up Women

Master the Art of Dating Women

Master the Art of Sex and Seduction

Never Good Enough – Escaping The Prison Of Perfectionism

No-Sweat Homeschooling – The Cheap, Free, and Low-Stress Way to Teach Your Kids

Psychic Vampires – Protect and Heal Yourself from Energy Predators

Reclaiming Your Soul – Healing Your Spirit, Building Confidence, Finding Your Voice

Reprogram Your Subconscious – Use The Power Of Your Mind

Signs From The Universe – How To Recognize And Interpret These Life-Changing Messages

Spirit Guides And Healing Energy – Worth Your Guides, Aura, and Chakras

Spirits I Have Known – Haunted Places, Haunted People

About Kelly Wallace

Kelly is a bestselling spiritual and self-help author, former radio show host, and has been a professional psychic counselor for over twenty years. She can see, hear, sense, and feel information sent from Spirit, the Universe, and a client's Higher Self.

She offers professional psychic counseling, caring guidance, and solutions that work! More than just a typical psychic reading or counseling session, you will feel you've found a real friend during your time of need—whether you simply want answers and guidance to your current worries or concerns, or you're interested in learning more about your soulmate, spirit guides, angels, past lives, or anything else.

Contact her today for an in-depth and life-altering reading!

Website: DrKellyPsychic.com

Email: Dr.Kelly.Psychic.Counselor@gmail.com

~ PART ONE ~

They're Everywhere!

Almost everyone has been the unwitting victim of a psychic vampire. It may have been a brief encounter with a stranger that left you feeling exhausted, agitated, or depressed, though the sensation may have quickly passed. Or, you might be the victim of a long-term energy drainer that seriously affects your mind, body, and spirit.

As long as there have been humans, there have been energy vampires. Rather than typical vampires like Dracula who live off the blood of people, the psy-vamp is far more dangerous. These predators feed off energy, leaving their victims drained, and they aren't often aware it's happening until it's too late.

Since these vampires are unable to produce their own energy system, they connect to another person's energies to recharge. Almost immediately the toxic person will seem full of energy while you're left mentally and emotionally depleted. The longer you're in the company of a psychic vampire, the more damage is done to your own system, sometimes leading to chronic depression, chronic fatigue, and a long list of other illnesses.

The psy-vamp can be young or old, male or female, and be in any line of work: from a secretary or dentist to a movie star or crossing guard. They can be strangers, friends, coworkers, neighbors, family members, or a spouse.

As we go through this book I'll share my encounters with various energy drainers. You may see many similarities to people you know now or have in the past! We'll cover ways to recognize these people, how to cleanse and protect yourself, and discuss why they do it and why you're so sensitive to their effects.

No longer will you be a victim. Instead, you'll be able to spot these people with ease and remain in total control of your personal power at all times!

Are You Being Attacked?

Everyone and everything puts out vibrations. Our thoughts and feelings are released into the air around us and others are affected by it. If you're generally a positive person you'll find that people, and even animals, probably like being around you. Without you speaking a word they may tell you that you've made them feel better.

They don't realize that they're absorbing your positive energy, and most of the time this is okay. You probably have some people you enjoy being around because they make *you* feel good, just as you benefit them with positive energy as well. Life is all about give-and-take, though it should be in balance.

However, I bet you know at least one person who takes far more than they give back. When this person is around your mood shifts and your energy levels plummet or become almost hyperactive. You might already know or suspect that you've been the victim of a psychic vampire, but do you have the kind of personality and the current type of aura that targets you as a victim? This quiz will show just how sensitive you are to these energy-draining people.

1. Do you often feel physically drained or sleepy after being around a friend or relative?

2. Is it hard for you to say "no" when someone asks for a favor?

3. Do people intrude on your privacy or personal time?

4. Do you often feel that people walk all over you?

5. Do you feel overwhelmed when in crowds?

6. Are you often asked to do the work nobody else wants to do?

7. Do you rush into situations with your heart rather than using your head?

8. Are you a people-pleaser, always setting your own needs aside?

9. Is it difficult for you to ask people for help because you don't want to feel like you're bothering them or don't want to be a burden?

10. Do you feel nervous interacting with others, especially strangers?

11. Is it important that you're well-liked by others and feel bad if someone doesn't seem to like you?

12. Do some situations make you feel so overly stimulated that all you want to do is lock yourself in your room?

13. Do you tend to get sick more often than others do?

14. Do you experience fatigue, dizziness, foggy thinking, and/or headaches though your doctor says there's nothing wrong with you?

As you looked over the list you may have answered yes to many of the above scenarios. If so, chances are you're a psychic empath; someone who's naturally sensitive to the energies of people, places, and things. Psychic empaths are particularly sensitive to psychic attacks.

Years ago, I would have said yes to nearly everything on this list! That doesn't mean we're weak, it just means we're psychically sensitive. We pick up on the subtle and not-so-subtle energies people give off. This is a wonderful gift but it's like having a magic wand and not knowing how to operate it.

The first step to reclaiming your personal power is to simply acknowledge that you're a very sensitive person. Once you realize this it's easier to begin working on cleansing and protecting yourself from these energy predators.

When I was first on this healing path I started being more observant of the types of people I interacted with. Which ones were sucking the energy right out of me or repelling me in some way compared to the people I enjoyed being around or could at least tolerate.

Before I left the house, I would create a strong spiritual field that would keep these psychic vampires from depleting my energy. In the beginning, it took some effort, but over time it became easier and now I can do this almost on auto-pilot.

Sure, occasionally a psy-vamp might slip in under my radar and I'll start feeling off in some way, but my higher self quickly steps in and makes me consciously aware of this. I'll then either excuse myself and move away from the person or, if I'm unable to leave, I'll mentally do a quick energy cleanse, create a barrier, and I'm in control of the situation once again. I'll teach you how to do this as well.

You don't have to give up who you are, and you don't have to be at the mercy of these vampires. After all, not all of them are bad, they just don't realize how draining they are to people like us. Won't it be wonderful to not feel bone-tired or frazzled after being around certain people? Won't it be empowering to finally be the one in control?

Signs Of A Psychic Vampire

Unless you live in a cave or on a deserted island in the middle of the ocean there's no way you can avoid psychic vampires. They're everywhere and they can be dangerous to those of us who are sensitive.

Complete strangers may gravitate toward you because on a subconscious level they're attracted to your energy. Friends, relatives, coworkers, or neighbors attach themselves to you with an invisible cord and keep coming back again and again for some of your life force. After all, if someone doesn't have enough life force of their own, where will they get it? From people like you and me!

By training yourself to spot a psychic vampire before they start sucking your energy away, you can tap into your higher consciousness and raise your vibrations so that you repel the psy-vamp and protect yourself at the same time. They'll have to leave you alone and find someone else to drain or learn how to recharge their own energy levels more constructively.

We'll cover various exercises later, but first, let's talk about the signs of a psychic vampire. Knowing what you're dealing with will help you protect yourself much better.

A Psychic Vampire Will Typically...

1. Seem more energized when around certain people

2. Prefer being with other people rather than alone

3. Keep conversations going (They talk things to death or repeat themselves)

4. Seek answers from others and avoid self-analysis

5. Ask others for favors a lot of the time

6. Be selfish and/or self-centered much of the time

7. Interrupt others when they're talking

8. Not be invited to parties or get-togethers

9. Prefer watching TV, playing video games, listening to music, or talking rather than quiet solitude

10. Have a strong personality

11. Feel perfectly fine in a crowd

12. Be the dominant partner in their relationships

13. Enjoy a lot of attention

14. Feel emotionally or physically tired

15. Need constant praise and reassurance

16. Complain, criticize, and/or gossip a lot

Now let's look at some things you might experience after a psychic vampire has drained you. These are the after-effects you deal with. Being in tune with yourself and noticing when you start feeling off in any way will allow you to move away from the situation or mentally repel the energy sucker the next time they're around.

Signs That You've Been Vamped:

1. You feel drained mentally, physically, and/or emotionally (This is the biggest clue)

2. After being with a certain person you experience self-doubt

3. You can't stop thinking about that person

4. You feel you should help them more than you do

5. You find that you make excuses for them (They're having a rough time, they're between jobs, etc.)

6. You start making their problems your problems

7. Your emotions feel out of control or you overreact

8. You feel depressed, irritable, moody, sad and it may stick around for a while

9. Things in your life start going badly or come to a complete stop

10. You start making mistakes at work

11. Things start breaking such as your car or computer

12. You keep talking to this person even though they make you feel very negative

13. You may feel physically ill or in pain after being around them

The closer you are to a psychic vampire the more difficult it is to see that they're attacking you. Who wants to believe that a spouse or close relative is making you feel so bad?

Ways To Protect Yourself

When you protect yourself from an energy drainer they'll either calm down and be more like you, or they'll leave because they subconsciously know they can't steal your energy.

1. When you know you'll be around a psy-vamp, ask your spirit guides and angels for protection and visualize yourself inside a white or golden protective bubble. No negativity can enter, and your energy remains intact.

2. Stay away from them if possible. I've had to abandon some longtime friendships because they were energetically harmful to me.

3. Use sage or incense to clear the energies in your home or car after the psychic vampire has left.

4. If someone makes you feel bad in any way and you don't have to be around them, don't! Your psychic gift is telling you this person is not good for you in some way so listen. Don't wait around until you see "proof" of their devastation before you finally get the message.

5. Keep yourself healthy and strong by eating more fruits and vegetables, leans meats (or other quality proteins if you're vegetarian or vegan). and other wholesome foods. Get some exercise daily, get enough sleep, and do a brief daily meditation. It's far more difficult to be drained when you're healthy.

6. Let go of any negative feelings the toxic person forces on you. Release it. Breathe. Smile.

7. Send this person healing light and happiness. They aren't usually aware of their effect on others. They may be weak, hurting, unhealthy, or out of balance in some way. By sending them positive energies you're ensuring your own protection.

Take back your power and refuse to let any psychic vampire make you miserable and tired.

Spotting The Psy-Vamp

As we just discussed, there are many ways to spot a toxic person who is out to deplete your energy. Besides things such as feeling tired, depressed, irritable, having a headache, or nausea, the best way to tell if someone is a psychic vampire is to watch them. By staying in the present moment and tuning into your feelings rather than what the other person is saying, you'll be more easily able to spot one of these drainers before they do any harm to you.

When you pay attention to them you'll notice that they take from others in greater quantities than they ever give. They complain a lot, the world seems to be against them, and they're often envious of the success of others. They're typically loud and opinionated and often have an opposing view and argument for anything you mention. They're usually irresponsible and blame everyone else for their problems and misfortune in life. They pick people apart, find fault with everyone and everything, and nothing is ever good enough.

This makes them sound awful to be around, doesn't it? And, very often they are. However, not all energy reapers are bad. They're rarely conscious of what they do to others. They simply feel angry or empty or down and need someone to talk to. Or, they might be looking for fun and call everyone they know trying to find someone who will go out and party with them. Most have no clue as to how to refuel themselves in positive and constructive ways. They're often misguided and usually have a lot of charm and potential, though it's typically wasted.

The psychic vampire will usually have low self-esteem, relationship problems, have trouble holding down a job, a poor body image, be chronically in debt, and swim around in their negative thoughts. The only way they can cope is by soaking up your positive energy.

It's incredibly important to your mental, emotional, physical, and spiritual health to choose wisely who you spend time with. Why waste your days with people like this? True, you might not always have a choice, but you do have complete control over who you give your energy away to.

One very quick way to ward off an energy drainer once you identify them is to visualize a loving, healing violet-colored light coming down from their spirit guides/angels. Send thoughts of love to this person as you visualize the violet light surrounding them in peace and healing. Just this one simple action can do wonders!

As you get better at strengthening your energy field and protecting yourself you'll find that negative people will start to drop out of your life and avoid you altogether. In some wonderful instances, your newfound power will empower them as well and this gives them the incentive to change their own world. This is a best-case scenario, though it does sometimes happen.

If there are a lot of psychic vampires in your life and/or these energy robbers tend to gravitate toward you, this is a clear indication that you need to work on your personal energy.

It may seem that I've overly dramatized the negative effects these vamps can have on you, but knowledge is power. I don't want to instill fear in you or create feelings of paranoia. I simply want to educate you and teach you how to protect yourself and live a positive life. Why waste precious time with people who bring you down?

Thankfully, we have an endless supply of energy. Yes, there will be times when you feel weak and drained and will need to replenish yourself, but a psychic vampire can't drain you so completely that there's nothing left.

What I hope to accomplish is to not have you fearful or overly concerned with these "poisonous" people, but instead to focus on yourself and becoming stronger. When you're living a positive, happy, healthy life you won't even have to worry about energy drainers because they'll have no power over you. They'll either avoid you or take some of your energy but you'll never notice because your supply will be infinite.

How They Use Your Energy

Everything puts out energy vibrations: people, animals, plants, even stones. As a human being, you give out various frequencies of energy depending on your mood and the aura boundaries you've set for yourself. These work together and can attract positive or negative people and events every day of your life.

Have you noticed in the past that sometimes, even though you might have been feeling positive and energetic, someone comes along and completely drains you and you're left feeling tired, angry, or depressed? That's because, although your mood was in the right state, your energy boundaries weren't. Without thinking, you were sending out a silent message letting psychic vampires know they could come and steal your energy.

And, regardless of the frame of mind you may have started with, the psy-vamp can get you to give out the type of energy *they're* craving. Think about the various energy robbers you know and the last conversation you had with one of them. Typically, they will get on a subject that will steer your energy levels in the way they need.

For example, you're talking to a toxic person and you don't know it yet, but they need anger to refuel. So, they might start talking about something they know will get you worked up, such as a person that owes you money, a run-in you had with your boss, or someone who did you wrong months or even years ago. They get you fired up so they can fire themselves up and replenish their depleted energy levels.

Over the years I've noticed that a lot of psychic vampires tend to party a lot or find some other way to be around a crowd. I've known many who love their Sunday church meetings because they know a lot of people will be there. They enjoy having a roomful of people. They'll naturally gravitate toward one person, drain them, and move on to the next victim.

Many vamps have outgoing and attractive personalities, and they use this to their advantage. They can make friends easily, spend a great deal of time with this new person, but when this "fueling station" is drained the vampire moves on to another new friend.

Energy suckers are also known for having various groups of friends that they rotate between, pulling out the energies of one or more people in the group then moving on to the next group. If a psy-vamp spends too much time alone they become incredibly tired and depressed or are bouncing off the walls. They need the energy of others to balance themselves out.

In a perfect world, we would all give out positive energy and enjoy receiving positive energy in return. The truth though is that positive energy takes time, practice, and conscious effort in the beginning and most people yearn for a quick fix.

We're all energy vampires sometimes and that's perfectly natural. Say for example you argued with someone you care about. You thought about it a lot and this greatly affected your energy field. If you could have seen your aura at that point it probably would have been red or black and extended several feet around you.

Anyone in the same room would have felt it! Perhaps there were people around and most avoided you (the ones who unconsciously protect themselves) and there may have been at least one person that approached you and tried to help you feel better. You might have talked a bit and in the end, you felt better. Perhaps you even laughed and smiled.

At that moment *you* were an energy gatherer. You were feeling down and drained or agitated. You then pulled the positive energy from the person trying to help you and things were in balance once again. This is the normal give-and-take all people should do. It's the toxic drainers that never give back and just keep taking that is the real problem.

Energy vamps are also great at pushing your buttons. They know just how to get a rise out of you. How to get you irritated or frustrated. When this happens, you begin putting out vast amounts of energy and the vamp greedily feeds off this. You could be left feeling angry and they walk away recharged.

They don't want to chase away one of their sources of power though so it's very common for this button-pusher to later contact you with a seemingly heartfelt apology. You calm down and forgive them and they know they can come on back when they need another energy fix. These are the people that constantly have drama in their lives.

Not all drainers create some sort of negative situation to steal energy. They can be perfectly happy, upbeat people, but they still need to recharge. People like this may tend to stay busy, talk to a lot of people either through text/phone or in person, and rarely want to discuss anything negative. I refer to these types as "sun vamps". Their sunny personality naturally attracts people. They laugh and joke a lot, and seldom are serious. I know one such sun vamp. He's been a friend for well over a decade and has the type of personality that draws people to him like moths to a porch light. Ask anyone and they'll say how much they love being around him.

The sad thing is, not one person has ever had an in-depth conversation with this guy and he never talks about anything negative. If you ask him how a tough situation in his life is going or want to talk about a problem you're having he'll quickly change the subject or suddenly need to leave. He has several groups of friends and rotates between them, unknowingly getting his "happy fix" from each group.

As far as life force drainers go, this type is the least harmful. It is sad though since he should be refueling his own energy tank rather than solely relying on others.

Everyone needs to recharge somehow. Without your energy field, you wouldn't exist. Your life force is what keeps you living and able to function each day. People who are suicidal have failed to replenish their aura energy. Without a constant flow of energy, you become more and more depressed until you either recharge or give up.

By understanding how your personal energy works and affects you and everyone around you, you can learn to protect yourself and avoid those negative energy drainers. Just because they need to recharge themselves by feeding off unwitting victims doesn't mean you need to be one of them.

Do They Need Willing Victims?

As we've been discussing, when one person takes more energy than they give back we label them as psychic vampires. Although this makes them sound evil, most of these energy drainers are completely unaware that they're doing it. They tend to be overly clingy, very needy, and oblivious to personal boundaries.

If you feel you've been the victim of an energetic vampire it's only because you've been unaware of their power over you or uncertain about how to ward them off and protect yourself. They can't drain people who are not willing victims. Anyone who refuses to take measures to deflect or avoid these types of people is open to being a victim. Why perpetuate such a negative situation?

Although most of these psy-vamps are unaware that they drain people, it's up to everyone to be in tune with themselves and their effect on others. However, it's rare when a drainer will take responsibility and learn how to energize themselves rather than relying on their habit of energy-robbing. Too many people are happy to get something for free rather than work for it! But it's also your responsibility to create personal boundaries and protect your energy space. You can't relinquish your power without permission.

So, yes, they do need willing victims, although you're probably not aware that you're actually inviting them to take your energy away from you. In many of my books, I talk about the law of attraction. In other words, what you focus on expands. Sure, you might not *want* to be drained of your energy, but you could subconsciously attract psychic vampires into your life. Creating strong personal energy boundaries and having a healthy aura are the best ways to attract positive people rather than those who deplete you.

Every person should be their energy source.

~ PART TWO ~

Your Psychic Antenna

Everyone is intuitive, some more than others. Right now, I want to show you how to fine-tune your psychic antenna. This will come in handy when trying to weed out potentially negative people from the positive ones.

So often we ignore that little voice inside us saying someone or something just doesn't seem right, or a person we know or have recently met affects us negatively. We want to believe most people are good and kind and will have a positive impact on our lives, so when that niggling sensation, that gut instinct that's telling you to avoid a certain person pops up, we squash it down.

What a mistake that is! By learning to tune into your psychic feelings you can avoid so many people that may eventually prove to be hazardous to your life.

Sharpening Your Intuition

1. The first thing I want you to do is to think of four different people you know. Choose one person you love, one who is fun and makes you feel energized, one who makes you feel angry, and one who is completely boring or low energy. These can be people you know now, have known in the past, or a mixture of both.

2. Now think about the person you love. Visualize how they look and sound, and how they make you feel when around them. Imagine some of the good things you've experienced with this person and notice any sensations as you do this exercise. You may

feel warm, excited, happy, and maybe even smile as you think of them. Notice *where* you feel this person. When I think of someone I love a lot I get a warm, tingling sensation in my upper chest area. I feel lighter, more relaxed, and at peace.

Make a mental note or, better yet, write down all the positive feelings you associate with this person, how they make you feel, and where you experience the sensations.

The reason I want you to focus on your thoughts and sensations is because you're honing your intuition when it comes to other peoples' energies. This will be incredibly helpful so you can attract better people and protect yourself from the negative ones.

3. Now close your eyes and take three deep, cleansing breaths. This will help you clear your mind and energy field of the person. After you've done that, open your eyes and think of someone who is a lot of fun to be around. Someone who makes you feel energized.

Just as you did with the *person you love exercise*, think of some fun times you've had with this other person. Visualize times when they've made you laugh, when you've done some wonderful things together, maybe a situation that got a bit crazy but was still very fun.

Where do you sense this person in your body and how does it feel? When I bring up memories of one of the most fun people I know, I feel a sensation in my stomach, almost like the energy is jumping. My head feels light and I automatically smile.

As you did before, make mental notes or write down a list of the feelings this person fills you with.

4. Close your eyes and take three deep, cleansing breaths then open your eyes. Now I want you to conjure up the image of someone who makes you feel angry or upset every time you're around them. This is usually a difficult person to focus on since they bring up so many negative emotions.

Maybe the person complains all the time, they might brag or argue a lot, or something else that just makes you feel negative whenever you think of them or have to be near them. What are the sensations this person causes in your body and where do you feel them?

Years ago, I had to be around someone quite often that I cared about because she was a friend, but she also upset me at the same time. She was always negative, always bragging, always making bad choices in life, then blaming others. I'd try to counsel her, offer guidance and even help many times, but she just wouldn't change.

Whenever I was with her I noticed I felt tense and often crossed my arms or legs, almost like I was subconsciously protecting myself. I'd come home feeling drained to the core. Finally, I had to cut her out of my life. It wasn't easy, but necessary. When I think of her even to this day it's like a heaviness on my shoulders. The sensation feels dark and sharp.

5. Again, close your eyes and take three deep, cleansing breaths then open your eyes. Let's focus on the last person on your list, the person you find incredibly boring. This could be someone

who rarely talks or has nothing positive to talk about. The two of you have little in common and this person never has much going on in their lives. They don't make you feel angry, just anxious to get out of their company.

When you visualize this person and some of the times you've been around them, what sensations do you feel and where? I remember one guy I used to talk with only because he was part of a circle of friends. I enjoyed most of the people, but this one man was just so boring to me. He'd sit there with a drink in his hand, talking about recent car repairs, his latest get-rich-quick project, wondering if he should switch his cat's food, and how he had chronic insomnia.

Normally, small-talk is perfectly fine, but this was all he ever did. He was a nice guy, but his energy just dragged me down. I could go from feeling on top of the world then like I'd just fallen off a cliff when around him. As I think of his energy I sense it around my knees and it feels like a tight belt around them. Odd, I know, but everyone will sense things differently.

Just as we did before, make the mental or physical notes of all the things this boring person makes you feel.

If you want, do this exercise for each person you know. You just might be surprised at how differently they affect you. Even some that you thought were perfectly fine, when you use your intuition to tune into them you may find that you have a different perspective.

That's how I feel now about a very high-energy friend I used to know. Everyone loved her. I thought I loved her too. After all, who wouldn't want to be around someone upbeat and energetic? I never realized how drained she made me feel though! I'd go home and want to take a nap. It was then that I realize she was a psychic vampire. She was so energetic because she was unknowingly draining everyone she came in contact with.

After that realization, I thought about the impact she had on my life. Was she so incredibly positive and such a good friend that I would need to learn to protect myself when around her while still enjoying her company?

A funny thing happened that made my decision for me though. I did some self-protection exercises each time before I was going to be around her. Her intuition must have picked up on this because she wasn't the ball of energy she usually was. Soon, she stopped wanting to be around me because she couldn't siphon away my energy for herself.

Now that you've been learning to sharpen your psychic antenna be sure to pay attention to any signals it sends you. As soon as you talk to or are around a person take a few seconds to tune into their energy and see how and where it affects you.

Even if you've just met them, you can get a good idea of how you'll feel about them and how they'll affect you by the sensations they create. Since you did this exercise and know where you typically feel love, joy, anger, boredom, etc. it will be easier to spot the type of person they are and if you want them in your life.

Some people might give off several different types of energy and you might not be able to pinpoint it at first. If you look deep enough and ask your higher self whether the person feels positive or negative, you'll nearly always get a quick response. Over time, without even thinking about it, your intuition will send you sensations and you'll pick up on it right away.

Stopping Them

Poisonous people can leave you feeling physically weak and emotionally down. It's a problem that won't go away as long as you're around them. Since they can't keep their internal energy going, they need to siphon it away from others. We just covered how to sense these people, but now I want to show you ways to protect and cleanse yourself. Most of these you can do anywhere at any time. All are very quick and easy.

Cleansing and Protection:

1. If you begin feeling "off" in any way this could be a sure sign that someone is trying to deplete your energy. Look at who you're with at the moment and try to identify the psychic vampire as soon as possible. By doing this you'll immediately empower yourself. Most psy-vamps rely on their victim being unaware that they're draining their energy.

2. Do your best to avoid being around any known energy drainers, or keep your interaction to a minimum.

3. If possible, stay away from negative environments where these types of people gather. Years ago, I had joined a crochet club. Sounds pretty harmless, right? After my third meeting with them and going home feeling irritable and drained to my very soul, I realized there were too many negative people in it.

Outwardly, they all seemed perfectly nice, but my intuitive alarms were going off like crazy and I stopped going. I felt like a load had been lifted from me!

4. Carry a black stone with you to protect against psychic attacks. Black tourmaline, which wards off negative energy, is especially good, but any dark stone will repel or dissolve negative energies. Other good stones are: Smoky quartz, hematite, jet, black onyx, black obsidian, and apache tear. I have several dark stones and usually let my intuition guide me when choosing which one to stick in my pocket. Keep the stone close to you since it works best being within your aura field.

5. Carry rose quartz which replaces negative feelings with positive ones. I like putting a dark stone in one front pocket and rose quartz in the other.

6. Take a daily shower since moving water helps to cleanse negative energy from your aura. Have you ever noticed how good you feel after a shower?

7. Keep your energy system strong by eating healthy, exercising a bit every day, drinking herbal tea, doing yoga or meditation, and surrounding yourself with positive people.

8. Each day before you get out of bed do a short visualization and affirmation, claiming your personal power. Close your eyes and imagine your aura all around you. It can be any color you like. Your higher self will know which color to pick.

Visualize your aura being bright and encompassing you completely. Then say out loud or to yourself, "I am empowered.

My energy belongs to me. I deflect all negative energy. I am strong. I am safe." Smile and open your eyes. Do this any time you feel your energy starting to dip.

9. Do all you can to make your life as happy and healthy as possible. Energy drainers find it difficult, if not impossible, to steal from positive people.

You never have to be the victim of a psychic vampire. You can do many things to block them and strengthen your energy field. You're far more powerful than you realize so put that power to work for you rather than giving it up to others.

Cutting Cords

It can be overwhelming when you realize how many people are energy robbers. We've already talked about how they can be members of your family, close friends, co-workers, neighbors, or people you interact with only briefly such as salespeople, cashiers, and so forth. In my own experience, I've noticed that at least half of the people I meet are energy drainers. Of course, I may be more sensitive to this, but it's more common than most people imagine.

By learning to cut cords you can keep yourself healthy—mentally, emotionally, physically, and spiritually. The exercise below is more in-depth than the previous quickies we discussed, but it's worth putting the time and effort into if you truly want to get rid of a chronic energy robber.

One of the most common traits about these psychic vampires—besides stealing energy from others—is that they tend to have a victim mindset. They feel that people are out to get them, that nothing ever goes right, that it's "every man for himself", or any other way of thinking that dis-empowering.

The only way they can make themselves feel better is by attaching themselves to your energy field with invisible wires. These wires act like extension cords that are plugged into an outlet—and you're the outlet supplying them with energy! Sure enough, whenever these people need a boost, they'll call you, visit you, or gravitate toward you in some way so they can get their energy boost.

As I mentioned before, the majority of psychic vampires are unaware that they're doing it and most mean you absolutely no harm. Even so, after you've been in their company they leave feeling great while you're left depleted.

These cords are also a two-way street. While they're taking your positive energy, they can unknowingly be sending you their negative energy. If that person was depressed, you may find yourself feeling depressed after being around them.

If they had a headache or stomach ache, you may start experiencing that as well. If they were worried or angry or anxious, you could begin feeling that way too. As you can see, these people can have an incredibly negative effect on your health.

It isn't all their fault though. Unconsciously you've allowed this person, or these people, to attach themselves to your aura field through these invisible cords. Think of all the negative people you encounter frequently. Those people that weigh you down and make you feel worse after being around them.

Maybe you only know one person like this, or ten, or more. Now imagine how many psychic cords are attached to you! All these cords siphon out your energy and prevent you from being your true self and living the life you desire and deserve. That's why it's so important that these cords be severed once and for all.

The first step in cutting cords from these people is to become aware of who they are and either avoid them altogether or limit your contact with them. Not being physically around them will help a lot, but psychic vampires don't even need to be near you to drain you.

A perfect example of "long-distance energy vampirism" is something in your past that still bothers you. This is especially true with traumatic episodes such as abuse. When you think of the person that treated you badly you may feel depressed, tired, sad, and/or angry. This is a prime example showing that the person has attached cords to you.

The second step is paying attention to your thoughts and feelings and consciously releasing all negative emotions. By holding onto fear, anger, hurt, jealousy, worry, etc. you're making yourself vulnerable to these energy stealers.

Just like a cold or flu virus sneaking in and making you sick because your immune system is currently weak, psychic vampires can sneak in and drain your life force if your aura energy is weak. Keeping your energy field healthy and strong will protect you.

The third step is to follow this cord-cutting exercise. At first, you should do this daily or even a few times each day when you're going through a particularly difficult time in your life. Once you begin feeling stronger and healthier, only do the exercise once a week or whenever you feel the need.

Cord-Cutting Exercise:

1. Go somewhere quiet where you won't be disturbed for at least 15 minutes, such as your bedroom. Sit on your bed, the floor, or in a chair. Close your eyes and take three deep, cleansing breaths through your nose, letting them out slowly through your mouth.

2. Mentally focus on each area of your body from your toes, all the way to your head, consciously relaxing each area. A good way to do this is to tense up each area as you focus on it then relax it.

3. When you feel relaxed ask your spirit guides or angels to help you in cutting all cords that are attached to your energy field. Imagine your guides cutting through these cords with powerful swords or lasers, dissolving them, and turning them to dust. The dust is then swept away, carried up into the universe where the guides and angels can transform any negative energy into positive energy It's great to have a team like that fighting on your side! Know that these cords are destroyed forever.

4. At this point you should feel some sort of shift, lightness, or other sensation letting you know that the cord-cutting exercise worked. If you don't feel any different that's okay, it often takes time to sever cords that have permeated your aura and grown deep roots. Have faith that the cords will be destroyed very soon. Ask your guides to surround you with a golden light of positive energy that will repel all negativity. I imagine this looking like a giant egg or bubble all around me and extending at least three feet.

5. Thank your guides for their assistance, take three cleansing breaths, and open your eyes. Stretch a bit before standing since

you might feel a bit lightheaded or disoriented when you first end the meditation.

Go about your day and pay attention to see if you feel any differently. I've had clients do this very simple exercise and they've reported back saying that it had such a huge impact on their overall state of mind and energy levels.

Not only did they feel happier and more energetic, but their mental focus increased as well. You'll probably find that you start attracting more positive people and opportunities too! It's amazing how incredibly powerful the human energy field is.

More Ways To Cut Cords:

1. Write down all your feelings of fear, anger, frustration, sadness, worry, or hurt regarding a certain person or situation. Keep writing until you feel you've gotten it all out. (I once wrote a 13-page letter to my step-father!) Don't give this letter to the person. Instead, burn the paper either in a metal bowl, sink, fireplace, or another fire-safe way. Imagine all your negative feelings being cleansed by the flames, the energy cords turning to ash.

2. Burn any pictures, letters/cards/notes, or objects that hold negative memories of a person, place, or situation.

3. Stop reading and watching things that make you feel negative or have any negativity attached to them. The current news headlines and so-called reality shows are two of the biggest energy suckers. Their sole goal is ratings, so they prey upon the

public by appealing to our sense of fear and our need to be entertained by drama.

4. De-clutter your home, office, and car. The less room you have for positive energy to circulate, the more negative energy will accumulate. Negative energy loves to make its home wherever there's an excess of junk, dirt or grime, and darkness. If you haven't used something in six months, get rid of it. Clean your house as spotless as possible. The better you feel about your surroundings, the weaker those cords become.

5. Light your favorite incense and carry it from room to room walking around the perimeters so the smoke from the incense can get into all the corners. Smoke is an excellent way to rid your home of negative energies. All those cords you've been carrying around have sent out a lot of negativity, filling the spaces you spend the most time in.

6. Listen to uplifting music. They say that music is the language of the soul and the vibrations from positive music can help in changing and strengthening your aura field and severing those negative cords.

The above exercises are all excellent tools in helping you to reclaim your personal power. I urge you to complete at least one of these activities every day for the rest of your life. Choose one (or more!) that resonates most with you at this time. Try others when you feel like it. As the days pass you'll begin to see how much more empowered you feel.

Spinning And Clearing

Here's a quick and enjoyable exercise you can do any time you're feeling bogged down by negative energies or want to recharge yourself after being drained by a person or situation. I learned this years ago from one of my psychic friends. We were at the park watching our kids play and run around. As we were talking I saw that her five-year-old son closed his eyes and started spinning around. My girls followed suit and soon they were all laughing.

A moment later they stopped spinning and went running off to play on the swings. I thought it was cute but didn't think much of it. My friend then told me, "Kids instinctively know what to do to rebalance themselves. They sleep when they're tired, eat when they're hungry, and spin when they need to recharge." We talked about this for a bit and it made perfect sense.

When a psy-vamp drains you, or you've had a stressful day at work or with the kids, your energy is very low. You might feel bone-tried and want to take a nap or you could have nervous energy. Your aura field is out of whack due to the draining effect of the person or situation.

When you spin it's like turning the crank of a generator; you're recharging your spiritual battery. You're strengthening and tightening your aura field. And you'll find that you feel much better afterward. Whenever I do this it makes me laugh, but also brings me inner peace, better focus, and energy.

Spinning Exercise:

1. Go someplace where you'll have plenty of room to spin around. This can be any place in your home, your yard, a park, the beach, etc. In the beginning, you might feel more comfortable doing it behind closed doors, but when you feel the benefits of spinning you might not care who sees you!

2. Close your eyes and imagine your aura all around you. This can be any color, and your higher self will automatically choose the color you need right now. Visualize your aura surrounding you like a bubble, encompassing you from head to toes.

3. Imagine your aura starting to spin around you in a counter-clockwise direction throwing off any negativity that's sticking to you. I like to imagine this negative junk flying off me like mud or oil, going into the universe where my guides and angels can transform it into positive light.

4. Hold your arms out to your sides and open your eyes to keep your balance. Start turning your whole body counterclockwise, just as you envisioned your aura doing so. Turn as many times as you feel comfortable with, but don't get so dizzy that you fall; 5-10 times is perfect.

5. Stop and take 3 slow, deep breaths.

6. Put your arms down at your sides and close your eyes as you now visualize your aura spinning clockwise, recharging itself, becoming stronger and brighter, spinning faster and faster. Maybe it's a different color now. Maybe it's the same color you saw just a moment ago, but now it's clean and bright.

7. Again, hold your arms out to your sides and open your eyes to keep your balance. Now begin turning in a clockwise direction 5-10 times, just as you did before.

8. Stop and take 3 cleansing breaths.

9. Put your arms down and walk around a little bit or sit if you feel dizzy.

Whenever I do this exercise I always feel refreshed, energetic, centered, and happy afterward. When I do it outside in a soft, safe place like on the grass at the park or sand at the beach I allow myself to spin a bit faster or longer. Have fun with it but do be careful. You'll not only release negative vibrations but will fill yourself with fresh energy.

If you're unable to physically spin due to your surroundings or if you don't feel safe doing it, feel free to stick to the visualization part of the exercise only. It will still do wonders!

The Vampire Returns

By now you realize how much you're affected by unseen forces. You don't need to see a virus or bacteria to experience the damage it can do when you come down with the flu, a cold, or an infection. Wind can't be seen, but the effects of it can be when there's a tornado.

The same is true of energy vampires. We can't see them sucking the energy out of us, but it can be felt. So far, you've read about cleansing and protecting yourself from these types of people and after some time you may feel that their effects were gone forever. But sometimes they return!

Perhaps you've cut the person out of your life and you don't see them anymore, or you've been doing your best to avoid them, but for some reason, they start contacting you or you begin thinking of them. The stronger the connection this person had with you—In other words, how much energy they could steal from you—often determines whether they come back. After all, you took away their "drug", their prime energy source, and they want it back!

A few years ago, I had done a lot of work on cleansing and healing myself from all the psychic vampires in my life—past and present. I was serious about it and diligent. Soon I was feeling better than ever. There were days when I felt nothing could stop me or bring me down. Then out of the blue one of my ex-boyfriends contacted me. Then another. Then another.

Three exes in one week? It wasn't a coincidence. What had happened is they sensed that they no longer had a connection with me. They weren't feeling that surge of energy when they thought about me. They began feeling drained and the only way to try to fill up their depleted tanks was to contact me and try to get me to interact with them.

I'll admit, I wanted to be a nice person so would be kind and send a short note back along with well-wishes. However, just that small amount of contact made me feel sapped.

So once again I did all my energy clearing and cord-cutting exercises and the next time they contacted me (and they did!) I deleted the emails without reading them. That made me feel bad at first, but then I felt empowered. I wasn't letting them into my personal space. Wasn't allowing them to drain my energy.

Sometimes these energy suckers will appear in your life when you're feeling weak, vulnerable, or stressed. When you get down on yourself or feel empty about something in your life you can subconsciously invite their connection back because some part of you may want it.

This is especially true of someone you've had a relationship with. We have those lonely moments where we long for someone in our life then begin to romanticize the past. You recall the good times you had, not all the things that lead to the breakup. It seems that the unhealthier a relationship, the stronger the psychic hold.

With one of my boyfriends, I was always suspicious about him cheating but could never find proof. My intuition was waving red flags all over the place though! Instead of breaking things off right when our relationship was destined for doom, I held on because I had no proof.

Over the following months, I started feeling more and more suspicious, depressed, obsessive, sad, tired, and my self-esteem was at an all-time low. A huge argument led to the breakup and nothing was ever resolved. There was never any closure. Although I did all the right things when it came to cutting cords and clearing and healing my aura, he'd always come back. He was my kryptonite!

One night I was lying in bed thinking of him (yet again!) and my higher self decided to step in and set some things straight. At that moment I finally recognized that we had a psychic connection because I'm very nurturing and he was projecting all his negativity onto me during the relationship.

I wanted to help him heal, but instead, I ended up owning all his junk—metaphorically speaking. All his insecurities, his low confidence, his depression, and the anger that he carefully hid behind a false persona of the "good guy" had been absorbed by my energy field, distorting my emotional vision and polluting my life. The cords between us were long and deep. Ugh!

Perhaps you've had a relationship in your past much like that—whether a lover, a friend, or relative. No matter what you do they keep coming back. It may be that they contact you, you run into them, or they suddenly and stubbornly pop into your mind or dreams.

Once you disconnect from them you'll feel the difference. The other person will most likely notice this too. They'll feel that something happened on a psychic level (even if they don't consciously label it as such) and know that it has to do with you. This is typically when they contact you because they *need* that connection. When this happens, you need to be very strong and own your energy rather than giving it away.

With people like this, you'll need to repeat the cord-cutting exercises several times before you're completely free of their draining energy. Even if you don't feel an immediate difference it *will* work. It may take some time and you might get to a point where you believe trying to clear this person out of your energy field isn't working, but that's only because you've gotten so used to the negative energy of that particular psychic vampire.

We get used to things as they are, even if it isn't healthy for us, and fool ourselves into thinking "this is just the way it is." That's why people who were abused in childhood often get into one dysfunctional relationship after another. Only when you break the connection will your patterns change, and you begin attracting more positive people and experiences. You can't cut those cords though until you're ready and willing to embrace a happier, healthier life.

Protecting yourself, your energy, and your space isn't being mean, it's being powerful.

~ PART THREE ~

Attracting Positive Energy

As a psychic counselor, I'm surrounded by my clients' energies daily. A lot of people come to me when they're feeling lost, frustrated, confused, depressed, or angry. As you can imagine, I need to constantly surround myself with positive energy so I don't absorb any negativity. Part of my job is to gather, use, and distribute positive energy to those around me. If I wasn't protected, I'd be like a sponge soaking up vibrations all day long and I wouldn't be able to think clearly or help people who come to me for assistance.

Although you might not be a practicing psychic, the energy fields of others affect you night and day—whether you realize it or not. So how can you block all this negative energy? Here are four powerful ways to not only combat any psychic vampires you may come across, but these are also excellent ways to surround yourself with positive energy every day.

Gathering Positive Exercises:

1. Earth Energy. The earth holds a special kind of energy that can almost be equal to our birth mother. In some instances, depending on how your mother is/was, Mother Earth can be even greater and more healing than your biological mother. The earth is very grounding and can help you release any negative energy that's built up in your aura field and will send you positive energy in return. Here are some great grounding activities:

- Walk barefoot in the grass

- Hug, lean against, or sit under a tree

- Sit on the ground and watch the sunset or sunrise

- Sit near a stream, river, lake, or on the beach

- Walk through a field, meadow, park, or forest

- Pick wildflowers

- Plant a garden

- Work with natural clay (You can make sculptures, pots, or just have fun with it.)

Whatever you choose to do, try to spend time in nature every day. You'll be rewarded with a cleansed energy field and will feel happier and more at peace.

2. Water Energy. Water is very cleansing to the astral body and is a powerful way to cleanse and change your emotions. If you're feeling stressed, depressed, or fatigued, water can easily change all that. Here are some ways to use water energy and cleanse your aura from negative vibrations:

- Take a shower

- Take a bath

- Swim in a pool or the ocean

- Walk barefoot in a stream or calm river

- Walk along the beach and let the waves ebb and flow around your ankles

- Drink a glass of water before every meal and when you first wake up

- Splash cool water on your face

- Run cool water over your wrists

- Play in the sprinklers (When was the last time you did that!)

Water will energize your body while calming your emotions. Enjoy the power of water each day.

3. Essential Oils. I love using essential oils for everything from headaches to sinus congestion. It's also wonderful at uplifting the spirit. When you're feeling more calm and positive it's much easier to release any negative energy you've absorbed and to protect yourself. Some of my favorite essential oils are:

- Clary Sage decreases fatigue, stress, and anxiety.

- Eucalyptus increases energy and mental clarity

- Lavender is great for calming, stress reduction, sleep, and headaches.

- Lemon, Lime, Grapefruit, or Orange are very energizing and uplifting

- Peppermint helps with alertness and stamina

What I usually do is mix one or two drops of any one essential oil with a teaspoon of carrier oil. You can use almond oil, olive oil, coconut oil, or whatever you have on hand. In a pinch, I've even used canola oil. I then rub a bit of the essential oil mixture on my wrists and temples. Within minutes I can feel the soothing or uplifting effects.

4. Fruits and Vegetables. Everything you eat has an overall effect on your body and spirit. Have you ever noticed how good you feel after having raw fruits or vegetables? That's because fresh, raw foods have positive vibrations—much more than cooked or canned. When you're feeling energetically drained or want to protect yourself daily from those psychic vampires, be sure to eat all the raw fruits and vegetables you can.

These four actions can be done daily in a very short amount of time—a shower, walk outdoors, a dab of essential oil, fresh fruits, and vegetables. From the first day, you'll experience tremendous benefits. Your aura field will not only heal and become stronger, but you'll also feel better and sleep better, have more energy, and you'll naturally ward off any energy-draining people.

You, The Psychic Empath

As we've talked about, the fact that you're affected by energy drainers is because you're a psychic empath. Because of this natural gift, you're intuitively sensitive to the moods and energies of others. Perhaps you "just know" when someone is in a negative mood even if they haven't said anything or they keep telling you they're perfectly fine.

You may see spirits out of the corner of your eye or sense them. You might get a feeling, a "knowing", that someone will contact you and they do. You could sense that driving down a particular street isn't a good idea, so you take another. There are so many ways your gift of intuition can pop up.

Until you learn to hone your psychic sensitivity and protect yourself it can often feel like a curse. After all, seeing or sensing spirits, having predictions that come truc, and dealing with people who feel as if they drain the very life out of you can be frightening. We go to school and learn math, reading, writing, and other subjects, but we're never taught how to work with our psychic abilities.

And so, people like us go through life wondering what's wrong with us, if we're freaks, being outcasts, feeling overly sensitive, and hoping that at some point this will all go away. But it doesn't. You can't hide from your natural psychic abilities. You must embrace them and learn to control your experiences rather than being afraid or having your experiences control *you*.

Although this book focuses on psychic vampires and how you can protect yourself from them, I urge you to begin working with your sixth sense today. The rewards will surpass any effort you need to put into this. You'll find that your confidence reaches an all-time high, you'll feel more positive, attract more positive people and opportunities, and those psy-vamps might not even come near you since they won't be able to get their energy fix from you anymore.

Here are a few easy things you can do to start embracing and increasing your psychic abilities.

Strengthening Your Psychic Abilities:

1. Be positive.

There's nothing that gets in the way of your natural intuition more than negative thinking. Have faith in yourself and release any skepticism. Trust that being psychic is as natural as breathing. Doubting yourself and your abilities will make you more susceptible to psychic vampires and you're just wasting something beautiful and valuable.

2. Meditate daily.

You don't have to do this for hours, I know I couldn't! Instead, setting aside 5-15 minutes a day can do wonders. Not only does meditation help release stress, but it's great for your physical health, increases energy levels, helps with mental focus, and gets you more in tune with your higher self and your sixth sense. The simplest way to meditate is to sit somewhere quiet, close your eyes, focus either on nothing at all or a positive image, and breathe.

3. Practice Peace.

To hone your psychic energies, it's important to be at peace with yourself and others. There's no place in your spiritual life for drama, arguments, grudges, and anger. Whenever you fill yourself with negativity it's almost impossible to think clearly, your problems seem worse, and you feel like you're being attacked from every direction.

4. Smile More.

Smile at everyone you come across; I bet they'll smile back. Happiness is contagious! Find constructive ways to expend energy such as pursuing a hobby, exercising, dancing, riding a bike, hiking, volunteering, knitting or crocheting, etc.

Do whatever makes you feel happy and content. Do more things that bring a smile to your face. Holding on to worry and stress gets in the way of your psychic talents; you need to feel spiritually free so you can reach a higher level of intuition.

5. Embrace Nature.

The Earth holds special energies that can help you increase your psychic abilities. Take a walk in a park, meadow, forest, by a lake, or near the ocean. During the summer I love to sit at the edge of the Patapsco River and take everything in. I inhale deeply smelling the scent of the trees, moss, water, and other living things.

My eyes take in the lushness of the leaves and vines, the softly moving water, the gray rocks, and the blue sky above. Nature is truly magical and we all have our favorite setting. One friend of mine loves taking walks in newly fallen snow, while another friend volunteers at a local greenhouse. Immersing yourself in nature can do wonders for the soul.

6. Use Oracle Cards.

Go on Amazon.com or to a local New Age store and look at the various tarot and other oracle card decks they have. There's something that will surely call to you. Whether you're attracted to fairies or angels, or are interested in traditional tarot, find a deck that appeals to you and buy it.

Don't read the little book that comes with the deck. Instead, spend time getting to know your cards. Besides any message on the individual card, look at the colors and symbols. What does each card say to you? How does it make you feel? Every day choose one card at random and really look at it then set it aside. At the end of the day see if you encountered anything that was represented in the card.

7. Keep Practicing.

Strengthening your psychic gift won't happen overnight, it will take a lifetime, but it's a wonderful and often amazing path to be on. Anything worth having doesn't come quickly. Even if you feel you aren't progressing as fast as you'd like, even if you have times when you feel you aren't psychic at all, keep practicing and believe in yourself. Over time you'll notice an increase in your abilities. Like any muscle, it takes exercise and daily dedication to strengthen it.

It's Up To You

I've done my best to show you how simple it is to cleanse and protect yourself from psychic vampires and strengthen your intuition. Although reading about it is helpful, the only way to prove that any of this works is to put it into action.

Reclaiming your personal power doesn't have to be difficult, take a lot of time, and it's never out of reach. All you need is to change your current way of thinking and viewing things, and spend just a few minutes each day practicing some or all the exercises I included in this short book.

I'd love to hear about your experiences. How did the exercises help you? Were you able to recharge your energy and deflect the psychic vampires in your life? How has your life changed? Where are you having problems? Would you like to book a reading? Contact me any time!

Dr.Kelly.Psychic.Counselor@gmail.com

Contact Me/Book A Reading

Whether your problems or concerns are in the areas of love, finances, family, career, health, education, or your path in life, I offer professional psychic counseling, and caring guidance.

I'll connect directly with your higher self and your spirit guides to help you through any situation and achieve the best possible results. No problem is too big or too small, and your questions will be answered in detail.

I'll let you know absolutely everything that comes through in the reading which typically includes past, present, and future energies, guidance, time frames and predictions.

All readings are done via email. By offering my readings through email you'll be able to save your reading and go back to it again and again for guidance.

I look forward to reading for you!

Check out my readings, books, blog posts, and more on my website:

DrKellyPsychic.com

Or email me directly at: DrKellyPsychicCounselor@gmail.com

9 781393 271406